My Pony Ride Business

*An inspiring story about responsibility
and young entrepreneurs*

Entrepreneurial Kids' Books

by
Dianne Linderman

Illustrated by
Dolores Uselman Johnson

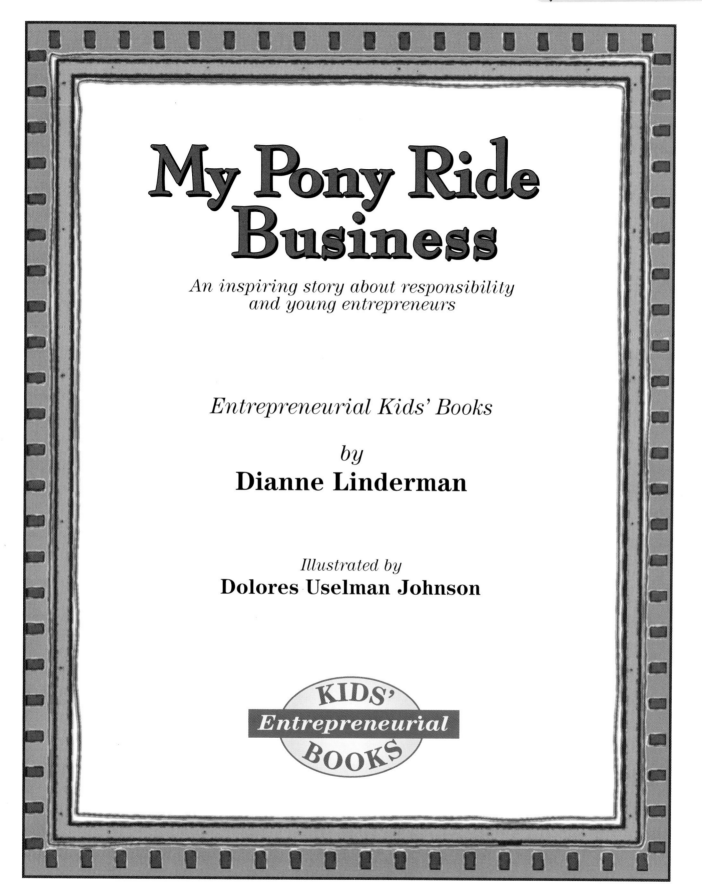

KIDS'
Entrepreneurial
BOOKS

Story by
Dianne Linderman

Illustrations by
Dolores Uselman Johnson

Edited by
Elizabeth von Radics

Layout by
Dianne Linderman and Saga Design

Library of Congress Cataloging-in-Publication Data
ISBN 0-9704876-1-4

Published by
The First Moms' Club
205 Fern Valley Road, Suite N
Medford, Oregon 97501
www.thefirstmomsclub.com

Printed in the United States of America.

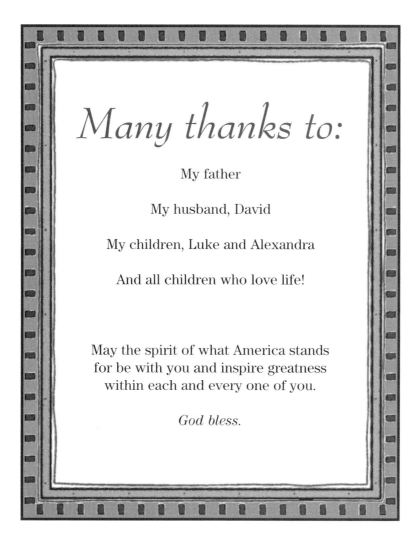

Many thanks to:

My father

My husband, David

My children, Luke and Alexandra

And all children who love life!

May the spirit of what America stands
for be with you and inspire greatness
within each and every one of you.

God bless.

B randon was ten years old and lived on a five-acre farm near a small town in the Pacific Northwest. He and his sister, Lauren, enjoyed helping their dad and mom with chores each day.

Brandon raked leaves, cleaned the barn, and fed the family's livestock. Lauren milked their cow, Daisy, and picked the vegetables and berries in the garden. She also kept track of where the hens were laying. Sometimes she had to hunt for the eggs, which she collected in a wire basket every day. She also took care of the barn cats, who took care of the mice.

One evening in late spring, Brandon was reading a book about ponies and how to care for them. He'd been wanting a pony for a long time.

His dad explained that ponies were very expensive to buy and that their care required both time and money. He said that if Brandon wanted a pony, he'd have to first figure out how he would pay for its purchase and upkeep. Dad reminded Brandon that he was a very good

worker: Why didn't he ask the neighbors if they needed a hand with chores? Brandon was so excited about the prospect of a summer job that he had a hard time going to sleep that night! He decided to visit the neighboring farms and offer his services the very next day.

SMITH MAIL

Brandon visited four neighbors, and two were willing to hire him. In fact, they were glad for the help! Mr. Smith hired him to mow the lawn once a week for $5. Mrs. Abigale said she'd pay him $2 a day to clean out her goat pen. She said that Lauren could help, too, by feeding her hens and ducks and collecting their eggs.

Brandon worked diligently for weeks. It was hard work, but it was also fun and satisfying, and his savings increased. One day he discovered that he had more than $100. He had finally saved enough money to buy a pony!

That afternoon he waited on the front porch, daydreaming about his pony, until his father came home from work.

"Dad! Dad! I've saved over a hundred dollars!" he exclaimed. "Can you take me to Mr. Eldon's stables to look at the ponies?"

Brandon's dad looked proudly at his son and said, "Let's get your mom and sister and go see what Mr. Eldon might have for sale."

The kids liked going to Mr. Eldon's stables. Brandon had taken riding lessons there the summer before.

ELDON
STABLES
← 3 MILES

Dad, Mom, Lauren, and Brandon climbed into their pickup truck and drove to the stables, which were just three miles down the road.

In his pocket Brandon had the money he'd worked so hard to earn. His long-awaited dream may just be coming true!

They pulled off the road, and Brandon jumped from the truck. There, grazing in the front pasture, stood the most beautiful Welsh pony he had ever seen. His eyes grew big, and he smiled.

"Wow!" said Brandon. "She's just what I've been dreaming of."

Brandon walked straight up to Mr. Eldon, shook his hand, and told him he was in the market for a pony. Before he knew it, Mr. Eldon had taken his offer of $118. With a final handshake, Brandon bought his very own pony.

Brandon was so excited! He wanted to ride his pony
home. His dad said it would be OK—so long as he was
very careful. Mr. Eldon kindly loaned Brandon a saddle,
so he mounted up and headed for home.

As he was riding along, Brandon thought about many
things. Would his current jobs bring in enough to pay

for the hay and grain? Mr. Eldon had said that he could work off the cost of the saddle by cleaning stalls at the stables. How long would that take? How would he repay Lauren for all of her help?

As his mind wandered, suddenly a loud noise spooked the pony, and she balked. Brandon almost fell off! He pulled himself up by the saddle horn and spoke softly to the pony to calm her down.

"Wow! That was scary!" he said. "I'll have to be more careful from now on."

When Brandon arrived at the barn, Lauren had the pony's stall ready and waiting. It was clean and dry, with soft hay and fresh water for the pony's first night in her new home.

"I've thought of a perfect name," said Lauren. "Peaches—because she's furry and cute!"

Brandon thought about how much help his sister had given him and thought it would be nice to let her name the pony. "I like that name," he said. "Peaches it is!"

d. Uselman Johnson

20

The next day Brandon was still wondering how to earn more money for his pony's care. He was hoping to think of additional ways, besides his current jobs.

After dinner the family sat down together to help Brandon figure out some ways to pay for the pony's upkeep. Lauren mentioned how much their friends will love riding Peaches.

"That's it!" said Brandon. "We'll sell pony rides!"

Dad agreed that at $1 each, ten rides a few afternoons a week would more than pay for Peaches's expenses.

"Peaches will love getting out and giving rides to kids," said Brandon. "She'll earn her keep and, with Lauren's help, I'll have my own business!"

Mom helped Brandon make a sign, and before bed Dad helped him nail it to the front fence:

PONY RIDES
MON. WED. FRI.
$1.00 per ride

The very next day, the neighborhood children were already lining up for rides.

Brandon was careful to give strict instructions about safety. He couldn't believe how much fun sharing Peaches and having a business could be. Peaches was bringing in more money than she was costing, so Brandon was even putting some in his piggy bank.

What excitement to have been able to put his hobby to work!

That evening when Brandon put Peaches into her pasture, he was in such a hurry to tell his dad and mom how much money he made on the first day of his pony ride business that he left the gate unlatched!

Before he knew it, Peaches had run out of her enclosure. "Brandon!" shouted his dad from a distance, "Watch out; she's loose!"

Brandon ran after Peaches and grabbed her mane tightly before she got very far.

Brandon's dad explained that having a pony takes great awareness and responsibility. "If you are going to have a business," he said, "you have to be responsible at all times—especially with animals. They depend on you for everything. If you are distracted, even for one moment, someone could get hurt. Having a pony is a huge responsibility and will teach you to keep on your toes."

Brandon learned a great lesson that day. He felt a little discouraged that he had been so careless, but his dad assured him that everyone has to learn his or her lessons in life. Some lessons are just bigger than others. His dad said finally, "Let's just be happy that you caught her so quickly!"

"On with life," said Brandon.

Brandon and Lauren continued to run the pony ride business, and word spread. Soon kids were coming from town for pony rides.

By the end of the summer, they had made some new friends and saved more than $200! To thank her for all her help, Brandon decided to buy a pony for Lauren.

"Just think, partner," he told her. "With two ponies we'll do *twice* the business!"

29

Brandon and Lauren are good examples of what hard work and simple ideas can bring about. If you put your heart into your ideas and follow them up with honest work, you can't help but succeed at anything you try.

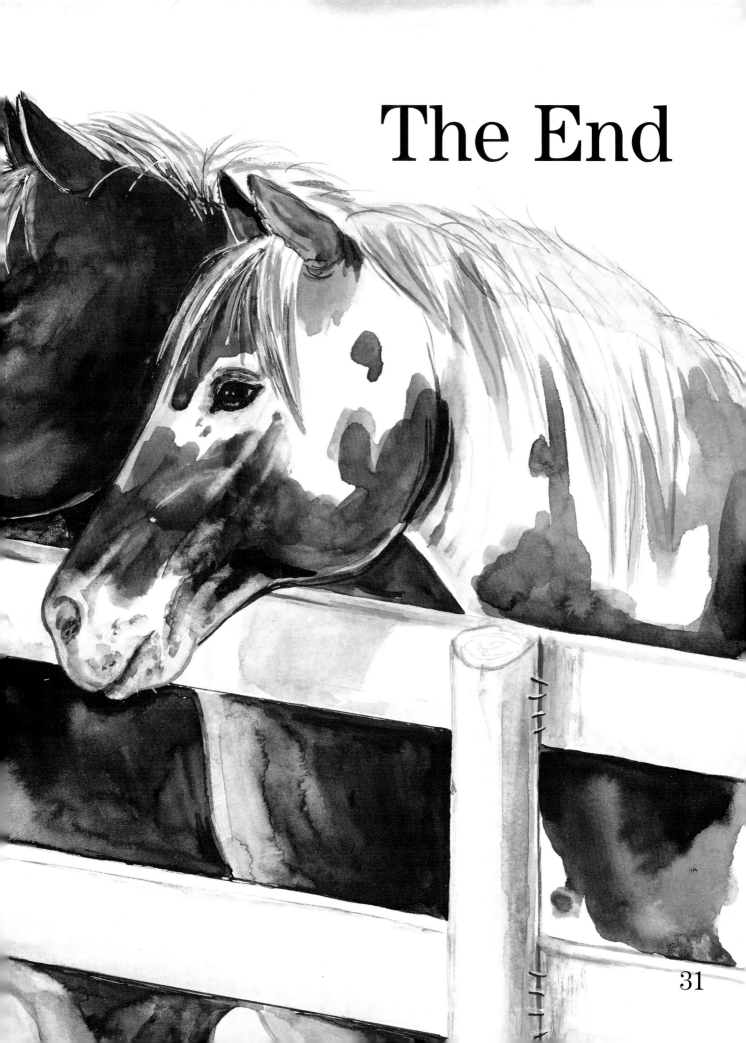

The End

Everything in life starts with one idea.

No matter how young children are, they can learn responsibility. Taking an idea from beginning to end takes responsibility, integrity, and character. Failures are just as educational as successes and should be made fun. I believe that inspiring children to be entrepreneurial is the best way to teach any academic subject. It gives them an appreciation of value and work and a reason to put reading, writing, and math to use. It also enables them to mature with character. Today's American youth are bored with meaningless distractions. We are losing the foundation of quality on which America was built. Let's plant their feet in fertile soil and let them blossom with self-respect, confidence, industry, and fun.

—Dianne Linderman